T0128634

Presented To

_____

With Love From

_____

On

_____

Dedicated to my Grandma Dorothy Mae
And my Baby Brother Theodore
- L.M.M.

AuthorHouse™
1663 Liberty Drive
Bloomington, IN 47403
www.authorhouse.com
Phone: 833-262-8899

Because of the dynamic nature of the Internet, any web addresses or links contained in this book may have changed since publication and may no longer be valid. The views expressed in this work are solely those of the author and do not necessarily reflect the views of the publisher, and the publisher hereby disclaims any responsibility for them.

Any people depicted in stock imagery provided by Getty Images are models, and such images are being used for illustrative purposes only.
Certain stock imagery © Getty Images.

This book is printed on acid-free paper.

ISBN: 978-1-6655-7305-4 (sc)
ISBN: 978-1-6655-7414-3 (hc)
ISBN: 978-1-6655-7306-1 (e)

Library of Congress Control Number: 2022918990

Print information available on the last page.

Published by AuthorHouse 10/21/2022

authorHOUSE®

WE MAKING! Yummy Things

EASY MEALS & TREATS. 7 DAYS A WEEK.

By

KRYSTLE H. MCCONICO

MONDAY

Hello, Everybody! I'm Lydia. Come with me and join in all the "Making" fun!

Meatless Mondays are so much fun! With lots of colorful veggies and rice, it gets the job done.

RICE & VEGGIE GOODNESS

What you will need:
* 1 Green Pepper
* 1 Yellow Pepper
* 1 Red Pepper
* ½ Onion
* A Few Mushrooms
* 1 Cup of cooked rice (Yellow, white, wild or brown rice! It's your choice! We like white rice with butter. :))

This is one of the easiest and most satisfying little dinners ever. Lydia exclaims, "All the vegetables are crunchy and yummy and making me strong, Mama!"

Clean & slice green peppers, red peppers, yellow peppers, onion and mushrooms.

Sauté them in unsalted butter until the peppers are soft, the onions are translucent and mushrooms appear glossy. Add salt & pepper to taste. Serve veggies alongside rice.

* Usually these two items with a sliced apple on the side are enough, but sometimes we add a cheese quesadilla to the equation to make a great meal even greater.

Tuesdays are for tacos, I must say! When I add in a green avocado, it really makes my day.

DECONSTRUCTED CHICKEN TACOS

What you will need:
Boneless, skinless chicken breast, chopped or shredded
*(If you really want easy, go grab a ready-rotisserie chicken from your local grocery store.)
Shredded lettuce
Shredded cheese
Pico de gallo
Seasoned black beans
Flour tortillas or white corn chips
Avocado
Lime

In the world of some tiny humans, they prefer their food to not touch
and we respect that. Lydia would put it this way, "Mama, I like all
this food, but I don't like it the way you and Dada eat it."

After cooking and seasoning your chicken the way you like it, assemble your
sectional dinner plate with your tiny human. Chicken, cheese, lettuce with a little
pico de gallo, cooked & seasoned black beans, sliced avocado with a pinch of salt
and a splash of lime. Corn tortillas can be featured later in the meal;). Yummy!

WEDNESDAY

Wonderful Wednesdays with its wonderful treats. My friends and I made ice cream; mango, chocolate and peach.

HANDMADE ICE CREAM - SHAKE AND NOT CHURN

What you will need:
½ Cup of Fresh berries, diced into small pieces
1 Cup of Milk *(We used Oat Milk)
½ Cup of heavy whipping cream
1 Tbsp. of pure vanilla extract
¼ Cup of sugar
Ice cubes
Salt
A large zip locked bag
A medium zip locked bag
A large food container with a lid
A large Cup (to prevent a huge mess:))

Pick a berry! Any berry! After your berries are cut into small pieces, place them in the medium ziplock bag. Pour milk, whipping cream, vanilla extract and sugar into the same bag and seal it. Fill large zip locked bag with ice cubes, a little over half the bag. Add salt on the ice cubes to prevent clumping. Place the medium bag inside the large bag and seal. Place the large bag inside the large food container and close. Shake for ten minutes. Yes! A true ten minutes of shaking and easy wiggle-exercise time! Lydia had some thoughts about this dual task, "Mama, I'm tired of all the shaky-shaking. I'm done now. Can we eat the ice cream outside and play?!"

Pour the ice cream from the medium bag into a serving dish and Yum:)

THURSDAY

On Thursdays I eat lunch from my purple lunchbox. A fun meal for my tummy plus dessert; a yellow cake pop!

POPPIN' CAKE POPS

What you will need:
One chocolate box cake; 9x13 prepared
Chocolate frosting
Melting wafers; dark chocolate or white chocolate
Apple skewers
Sprinkles
A Styrofoam block or Glass Jar filled with dry rice

Cake Pops-A Poppin'! Poppin' Cake Pops! Cake Pops-A Poppin'! Poppin'
Cake Pops! Lydia proudly sang this song as she headed to her last
day of PreK to give all her friends the cake pops she made!

After you've baked your box cake and it's cool, add it to a large bowl and crumble it up into fine crumbs. Add in two big spoonfuls of frosting. Mix with your hands until the cake is moist, can hold a ball shape, but it's still crumbly. Begin forming the mixture into a tight balls and place them on a plate. Place about five chocolate wafers in a small bowl and microwave for 30 seconds at a time until chocolate has melted. Be careful when melting because you don't want the chocolate to burn. Dip the pointy tip of the cake pop sticks into the melted chocolate and insert into the cake balls. Freeze for about 30 minutes.

Remove cake balls from the freezer; about five at a time. Melt the remaining chocolate in a large bowl. Carefully submerge the cake ball in the chocolate, then spoon the chocolate on to cover any bare spots. Let the excess chocolate drip off. Add the sprinkles while the chocolate is still wet. The chocolate will harden quickly so already have your decoration idea ready to go! Stick the decorated cake pop into a styrofoam block or into a cup of rice to allow time for drying. Place cake pops in the freezer again to speed up setting time.

Melt more chocolate of a different color to design the cake pops
and take it up a notch!! Place individual cake pops in clear, treat
bags & add ribbon for gift-giving and cake poppin' fun!

Forever a Friday with its flavorful cupcakes. Will I make strawberry, cookies and cream, pumpkin or grape!?

CUPCAKE CUTIE (icing)

What you will need:
Your favorite box of cupcake mix
2 Cups heavy whipping cream
1/2 Cup salted butter
1 Cup confectioners' sugar
1/2 teaspoon vanilla extract
1/2 teaspoon almond extract
1/2 Cup seedless strawberry jam
Pink food coloring
Fresh strawberries

We LOVE trying different cupcake icing flavors!! Lydia loves purple and she also loves seeing the icing colors change! Use the same steps below but, instead of jam, pink food coloring & strawberries use a couple drops of our favorite food coloring, purple, and top with grape flavored sprinkles or purple sanding sugar! You're welcome!

In a large bowl, beat cream until it begins to thicken. Add butter, confectioners' sugar, vanilla, almond extract and jam and; beat icing until you see little peaks stiffening throughout the bowl. You can either spread the icing or pipe it over the cupcakes. Store the remaining icing in the refrigerator. Lastly, slice up your fresh strawberries to garnish each cupcake to make them nice and ....cute:)

SATURDAY

Saturdays are the best because we slow down the pace.
After lots of morning cuddles, we enjoy sprinkle pancakes.

THE PANCAKE ADVENTURES

What you will need:
2 Cups of all purpose flour
1/2 teaspoon salt
1 teaspoon of baking soda
3 Tbsp. granulated sugar
1 teaspoon vanilla
1/2 teaspoon of almond
2 eggs whites
2 Tbsp. melted butter
2 ½ Cups of low fat buttermilk
Sprinkles

Whisk egg whites and buttermilk together in a medium bowl until it stiffens. In a separate bowl, sift and mix flour, salt, baking soda and sugar. Fold in your egg whites and buttermilk mixture. Add butter and both extracts and let the pancake fun begin (Keep mixing up your pancake batter but, don't over mix it, ok)! Add butter and oil to coat the bottom of your frying pan and place over medium-high heat. Your batter should rest as the pan heats up. We make breakfast an adventure by using fun pancake shapers to make pancakes shaped as pirates, hearts, bunnies, dinosaurs or the good ole' state of Texas! You pick! BUT.... Don't forget to add the sprinkles to the wet side of the pancake as it's frying! Once the bottom side is golden, flip and brown the sprinkled side. Serve with syrup and truly, have the best day ever.

Sunday Funday! I thank the Lord!
There's so many recipes for me to explore.

I love cooking with mommy for family & friends,
making memories to cherish forever. The End.

MY, MY! APPLE PIE

What you will need:
Pie crusts
7 to 8 apples green apples
1/2 Cup brown sugar
1/2 white sugar
1/4 teaspoon fine sea salt
1 teaspoon ground cinnamon
1/4 teaspoon freshly grated nutmeg
1/4 teaspoon ground ginger
1/4 teaspoon ground cardamom
1/4 teaspoon ground allspice
2 Tbsp. cornstarch (or you can use 4 Tbsp. of flour)
1 Tbsp. butter
1 egg

We saved the very best for last! Peel and cut your yummy, green apples and place them in a plastic container. Mix the sugars, salt, cornstarch and all the spices together then scatter them over the apples. May no apple slice go uncovered! Set them to the side for one hour at room temperature. Preheat the oven to 420 degrees. Place your pie crust inside an oven-safe pie dish. Fill the inside until the apples are the same height as the edge of the pie crust. Pour all the apple juices at the bottom of the bowl over the apples. It should be about ¾ a Cup. Dot the pie with butter. Add top crust. We get fancy and lattice our top crust! Its pretty simple. Try it! Seal off the edges. Whisk egg with a tablespoon of water and use it as an egg wash on top of the crust. Put aluminum foil on the edges for the first 20 minutes so the edges won't burn. Bake the pie on lining paper for about 75 minutes. Please, please be sure to cool the pie without slicing into it for at least 1 hour or longer. So amazingly yummy and our family favorite!

MY FAMILY RECIPE

List the ingredients and each step of your favorite, family recipe.

_____
_____
_____
_____
_____
_____
_____
_____
_____
_____
_____
_____
_____
_____
_____

MY FAMILY RECIPE

List the ingredients and each step of your favorite, family recipe.

_____

_____

_____

_____

_____

_____

_____

_____

_____

_____

_____

_____

_____

_____

_____

_____

_____

MY FAMILY RECIPE

List the ingredients and each step of your favorite, family recipe.

_____

_____

_____

_____

_____

_____

_____

_____

_____

_____

_____

_____

_____

_____

_____

MY FAMILY RECIPE

List the ingredients and each step of your favorite, family recipe.

_____

_____

_____

_____

_____

_____

_____

_____

_____

_____

_____

_____

_____

_____

_____

_____

WE MAKING! Book Series:
Yummy Treats 7 Days a Week!
Arts & Crafts 7 Days a Week!
Music 7 Days a Week!
Big-Little Disciples 7 Days a Week!
And For More Fun, Please Follow @_Wemaking

Printed in the United States
by Baker & Taylor Publisher Services